FARMING IN F

Photographs of Leicestershire A
1860-1940

Leicestershire Museums, Arts & Records Service
1989

Leicestershire Museums publication no.100

Designed by Leicestershire Museums Design Section

Typeset by Typesetters (Birmingham) Limited

Printed by de Voyle Leicester

All rights reserved. No part of this publication may be reproduced, stored in a retrieval system, or transmitted in any form or by any means, mechanical, photocopying or otherwise, without the prior permission of Leicestershire Museums, Arts & Records Service.

© Leicestershire Museums, Arts & Records Service,
96 New Walk, Leicester, LE1 6TD, 1989

ISBN 0 85022 255 9

Cover illustration: **1.** The mower.

Foreword

These photographs have been assembled as part of Leicestershire Museums, Arts & Records Service's celebration of British Food and Farming Year 1989. By coincidence, 1989 is also Museums Year, being the centenary of the formation of the Museums Association; and it marks the twentieth anniversary of the opening of the Rutland County Museum, whose important agricultural and rural life collections are part of the Service. Most of the photographs in this book were also included in an exhibition which toured Leicestershire Museums during the year.

The photographs are from the collections of Leicestershire Museums, including those of the Rutland County Museum and the Harborough Museum. Together, these are effectively the county's own photograph album.

If you have any old photographs of Leicestershire, including Rutland, we should be pleased to see them, with any details you can supply. With your permission, our photographers would copy them so that they could be added to our record of the past, the originals being returned to you.

If you can help, or would like further information about our photographic holdings, please contact Leicestershire Museums.

We gratefully acknowledge permission from Brooksby Agricultural College to reproduce photographs 40 and 41.

Compilers: M E Ball, T H McK Clough, J A Legget, S Mastoris.

Introduction

The photographs in this book cover a period of some eighty years from 1860 to 1940. During this period, farming techniques changed radically from virtually complete dependency on manual and animal power to the facilities of a machine age. Rural prosperity ranged from the stability of the mid-Victorian era to the depths of the agricultural depression at the turn of the century. The appearance of the landscape varied over the years from arable to pastoral, while the crops grown and the stock bred also changed.

The photographs reflect some of these changes, but perhaps more importantly they also record a form of agriculture which has since virtually disappeared from Britain, and can now be found only on the poorest farms of temperate Europe. For in the half century since the outbreak of the Second World War, when our story ends, a further and even more far-reaching revolution has taken place in farming.

Today, haystack and rickyard are but memories in black and white. The smoke and dust of steam engine and threshing tackle have long since cleared away, and the heavy horses which pulled the reaper-binder have been replaced by a machine which does all these jobs, the combine-harvester. The varied greens of pasture and hedge have given way to the browns and golds of ploughed land, ripening cereals, and muddy sugarbeet. The springtime air no longer carries the sweet scents of meadow flowers. Instead, it is heavy with the yellow odour of rape fields and the sounds, not of harness, busy insects and birdsong, but of diesel engines and explosive birdscarers. Men plough not only in the dawn but also at night by the light of tractor headlamps.

Gone too is much of the back-breakingly heavy labour of the farm: lifting huge sacks of seed or potatoes weighing a hundredweight (112 lb or 50 kg) or more; steering the plough; cutting hay or reaping corn with scythe and sickle; turning the handles of root choppers, chaff cutters, or butter churns - or mangles on washday. It is commonplace now to regret the passing of traditional rural ways of life, but not everything was better in the good old days.

With these images in mind, it may come as a surprise to read accounts of the state of agriculture some 80 years ago. "The complaint of the deterioration in the quality of the work done is loud and deep. The modern agricultural labourer ... cannot compete with the old one in the better class of farm work, such as stacking, thatching, &c., and few take any pride in their work, though there are still a considerable number of the older men who can lay a hedge and shear a sheep well" (*Victoria County History, Rutland*, vol I (1908) pp 248-9). What, then, did these older men remember? What had the agricultural labourer to look forward to?

In the 1860s, both Leicestershire and Rutland were counties of mainly small farms. The quality of the land varied from one area to another. It was not hard to find poorly drained land, full of tussocks, weeds and anthills. New fences, hedges and rights of way had already completely changed much of the rural landscape, and few parishes still awaited enclosure.

The balance between pasture and arable differed

according to soil type and topography. Dairying was strong in west Leicestershire, with milk for neighbouring urban centres and Leicester cheese being produced by farmers with perhaps 20 or 30 cows. Pigs were bred and fattened, but sheep were not of great importance. Mixed husbandry was more prevalent in the north-west.

The south of the county, with its rich pastures, was a great meat producing area, so much so that many farms had little or no arable. Usually, cattle would be bought in the spring, perhaps after wintering in Norfolk, fattened through the summer, and sold in the autumn. Sheep were bought in the autumn, wintered on root crops, and sold in the spring, with their lambs being kept until the next autumn.

In central Leicestershire, there was more mixed farming, with perhaps a third of the land being arable. Around Melton Mowbray dairying was important, with Stilton cheese being a profitable commodity; fattened on whey or buttermilk, pigs, and consequently pork pies, were also common.

In Rutland, the picture was rather different. Almost half the county was arable, and in the east its lighter soils produced fine barley crops, much of which went to brewers for malting. Where the emphasis was on pasture, dairying was important. Sheep were universally plentiful, for they wintered on the turnip fields which formed part of the arable rotation. For example, the Board of Agriculture recorded in 1867 that there were 12,917 cattle, 109,726 sheep and 5,918 pigs in Rutland.

In both counties, growing root crops, especially turnips and swedes, accounted for a large proportion of the arable land. Potatoes, cabbage and vetches were also grown, but carrots, for example, hardly figured at all. Wheat and barley were the most important corn crops, followed by oats, beans and peas, and a small amount of rye.

Grain was probably sown using seed drills, except for awkward fields which might still be sown by hand. Growing crops would be weeded by hand or with a horse hoe. Reaping machines and portable threshing machines were becoming more common, and threshing contractors were setting up in business. Wooden ploughs were yet to be found, but the new generation of wholly iron ploughs had caught on fast.

On pasture land, there were some hay-making machines, but on the smaller farms, grass was usually cut and turned by hand. Everyone turned out to make hay while the sun shone, for a good supply of winter feed for dairy cattle depended on a successful crop. In the fields, the older men would be wearing their smocks, and the women their sun bonnets.

Farm buildings themselves were often old, inadequate, and in poor condition, except where landowners had expended capital in providing new ones. Where there were larger estates, they were often in the hands of progressive landowners. Model farms were set up, with ranges of new buildings and professionally designed farm workers' dwellings. Allotment systems were established, providing vegetable gardens for the workers.

Foremost in this field were men like Lord Berners, of Keythorpe in Leicestershire. Here, on a mixed farm of 850 acres, he drained the land, introduced steam cultivation, and installed the latest machinery in the barns, using spare steam to heat the floors to dry the corn; the whole premises were lit by gas.

In Rutland, similar advances were being made on great estates like those of the Earl of Gainsborough, whose agent R W Baker had married into the Ransome family, manufacturers of agricultural machinery. Where such sound advances in farming were being made, they would help a little to ease the disastrous effects of the impending agricultural recession.

From about 1875, a great depression set in. Grain, especially wheat, fell in price steeply as a result of foreign competition. Arable farmers and millers were hard hit. Farm rents fell, often by 25 percent or more, and many went bankrupt. In 1879-80, a disastrously wet season caused extensive outbreaks of liver rot amongst sheep, and many cattle also died of it. This, together with the effects of imported frozen mutton, started a great decline in the number of sheep in the east Midlands.

Dairying became more important as towns continued to grow. To meet the demand, more land was turned over to pasture. There was a drop in arable acreage of up to a quarter, with the emphasis on growing fodder crops for livestock. More hay was grown as well. By 1905, the livestock figures for Rutland were 19,429 cattle, 73,917 sheep and 2,232 pigs. The number of horses was virtually unchanged at 3,196. Amongst cattle, shorthorns were the favourite kind, and Lincoln sheep were well-liked.

Most agricultural land was farmed by tenants. The average holding was less than 100 acres, of which the smaller ones were worked by family labour alone. Perhaps a tenth of agricultural land was owner-occupied.

By 1908, then, older men were looking back over 30 years of depression. The outlook for agriculture was less gloomy. Produce prices were showing signs of rising at last, and greater prosperity seemed a possibility. However, the farm labourer of the day could hardly foresee the drastic changes which were shortly to come.

The outbreak of war in 1914 led to great pressure on the farming community to produce food. The trend away from arable farming was reversed, and some 10 per cent of permanent pasture was ploughed. By the end of the war, the first tractors had appeared. Some were made in Britain, but there was a great influx of American-built machines. Soon, these were to dominate the market so much that most British tractor manufacturers went out of business.

The Great War was followed by a severe economic depression which affected industry, commerce and agriculture alike. By 1930, pasture had reverted to its pre-war extent, and it continued to increase until the beginning of the Second World War in 1939. This war too was to have a drastic impact on farming and on the appearance of the rural landscape, and trends were set in motion then which were to achieve the development of agriculture far beyond the dreams of the rural labourer of the turn of the century.

The Horse - Source of Power

Men relied on their horses to cultivate the land. Although farm machines were invented or improved, the power of the horse limited change. It was the internal combustion engine that revolutionised agriculture.

2. Four horses, here harnessed in tandem, could plough little more than one acre a day on Leicestershire's stiff, heavy clays.

3. William Pepper farmed at Mountsorrell from about 1877 to 1941. Heavy horses like those pulling his all-purpose cart are still superior to tractors on some difficult ground.

4. There were about fifty blacksmiths in Leicester at the beginning of this century. One of them was Benjamin Herbert, here shoeing a grey at the Mitre and Keys, about 1910.

5. Mr Ferryman holds the head of a stallion while the owner, Mr Harrison, looks on. The photograph was taken near Lutterworth in 1880.

Cattle - Dairy Produce and Beef

Cattle were Leicestershire's most important livestock, their numbers increasing during this period. Dairying became more important than beef production as increased urbanisation led to great demands for milk.

6. The cows of a family smallholding amble tranquilly along the main street of Braunston in Rutland at milking time, some fifty years ago.

7. Prize-winning cattle bred on one of Rutland's great estates pose for the camera. Taken by the medieval motte-and-bailey castle of Mount Alstoe, near Burley-on-the-Hill.

8. A cowman, probably from Marston Trussell, near Market Harborough, in 1861. He is wearing the long smock-frock and heavy hobnail boots typical of farm workers throughout the 19th century.

9. Cattle in the High Street, Market Harborough, in about 1890. The weekly livestock market was held here and in the Square, formerly known as the Sheep Market, until 1903.

10. The dairy of a farm at Newbold Verdon. Scrupulous cleanliness was essential if the milk was not to be tainted or turn sour.

11. The Stilton Cheese Fair was held at Melton Mowbray three times a year from 1883. Although made in Rutland and east Leicestershire, Stilton retains the name of the village where it was sold to travellers on the Great North Road.

12. The humane killer was introduced to ensure painless slaughtering. Here, the new technique is being demonstrated to young butchers by Joseph Smith of Victoria Road East, Leicester.

Sheep - Wool and Mutton

Sheep were kept in very large numbers until the 1880s, particularly in eastern Rutland. Then, when the importation of frozen mutton began, their numbers dropped dramatically in both Leicestershire and Rutland.

13. A farm labourer and boy drive a flock of sheep along the road at Frisby-on-the-Wreake in the summer of 1927.

22. The Wild family of Hambleton, Rutland, recorded some of their farming activities on film. Here, Bonnie is in the haysweep, working to clear the hay harvest.

23. Haymaking in the Enderby area in 1859. All available labour was needed to ensure that when the hay was dry enough it could be stacked as quickly as possible.

24. A Fordson tractor driving a Bamford hayloader. Although the tractor had replaced horses, men were still needed to stack the hay on the waggon.

25. An agricultural labourer poses with his hayrake, no doubt a welcome break from the hot work of haymaking.

26. Carting and stacking hay was heavy labour. The size of these stacks shows the amount of work that could be achieved by manpower alone.

Arable Farming

Rutland was famous for its malting barley, but otherwise almost all crops were grown to feed livestock. Only 18 percent of Leicestershire's farmland was arable in 1939, but in Rutland the figure was 33 percent.

27. A haystack and cart, probably near Marston Trussell, in 1856. The wooden fencing around the haystack prevents animals from grazing it.

28. Autumn ploughing with two shire horses. Deep ridges were left for winter frosts to break the clods ready for spring sowing.

29. Spring sowing with a horse-drawn drill. Coulters cut drills in the ground, and seed drops into the drills from the funnels behind the coulters.

30. By the early 20th century, the reaper-binder had largely replaced the old method of reaping by hand. This machine could cut up to an acre per hour.

31. This giant 25 horsepower Mogul tractor, made by the International Harvester Co of Chicago, was imported during World War I.

32. Stooking wheat in about 1896. When the corn had dried, the sheaves were carted to the barn or rickyard to await threshing.

33. A remarkably late barley harvest after a wet autumn was gathered on Cooper's farm at Sewstern on 31st December 1907 and New Year's Day 1908. The harvesters huddled in their coats round a fire for their dinner.

34. A good harvest at Wartnaby. The size of the thatched ricks can be judged by comparing them with the man carrying a ladder.

35. The slow, exhausting work of threshing with a flail to separate the grain from the straw and chaff. This photograph was taken late in the 19th century.

36. A threshing machine at work in about 1940. The machine is powered by a steam engine, just visible behind the pile of straw.

37. Mr Coverley, about to lift a sack of grain, framed in the doorway of the watermill at Ratcliffe-on-the-Wreake.

People and Places

A flight from the land took place throughout this period, but for those who remained, the pattern of rural life continued almost unchanged until the outbreak of World War II.

38. Windmills, like this post mill, mostly fell into disuse at the end of the 19th century. Belvoir Castle stands on the skyline.

39. The farmer's wife feeds her hens at Newtown Linford in 1908. The sale of eggs and of butter gave her extra money.

40. Pigs were commonplace on farms and smallholdings until recently. Here a student feeds young pigs at Brooksby Agricultural College.

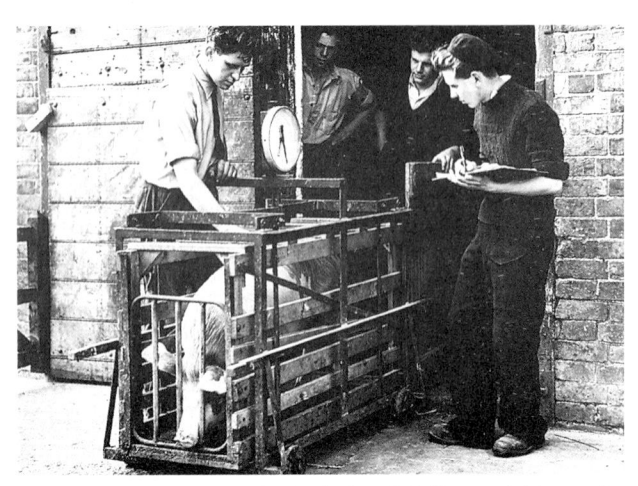

41. Students at Brooksby Agricultural College weighing a pig. Formal training has now become normal for all farmers and farm employees.

42. The family pig was an important source of food. In the 1930s, Mr Townsend of Edith Weston, Rutland, had his pig killed and butchered by Ernest and Elijah Tibbert.

43. A farmyard at Wing, Rutland, in 1915. The effects of thirty years of agricultural depression are apparent in the air of general decay.

44. Time for a mid-afternoon break in the spring sunshine at Fountain's woodyard at Greetham, Rutland, on 16th April 1914.

45. A woman knitting outside her cottage in the Enderby area, about 1860. Cottages like this were still inhabited at the end of the 19th century.

46. Thurcaston's wheelwright at work in his yard in 1910. The wheelwright was one of the most skilled craftsmen.

47. A study of two blacksmiths. The blacksmith was the most important village craftsman, for he made the tools used in agriculture and in other rural trades.

48. Fellmongers drawing skins from a limepit at the yard of George Staynes, tanners and leather dressers, of Market Harborough, in about 1870.

49. A girl strips the bark from a willow wand at Thurmaston's osier beds, about 1904. Willow was made into all kinds of baskets.

50. Stout, well-laid hedges were essential to fence in livestock. Here a hedger shapes a stake with his billhook.

51. A labourer fetches water from the village pump at Braunstone. The yoke with its pails was also used to carry other loads like potatoes or apples.

52. Members of the Rutland Young Farmers Club at Oakham Cattle Market, soon after the club's formation in about 1930.

53. R & E Bell of Market Harborough could supply anything a farmer might need, from American harvesters to barbed wire.

54. Homeward bound! A free arm meant that you could collect faggots for kindling as well as carry a basket.

Photograph references

The following list of photographs and reference numbers will enable the photographs to be identified within the Leicestershire Museums, Arts and Records Service's collection in the event of enquiries being made about them.

1.	A5510	19.	H4/01	37.	A9627
2.	A5506	20.	H1681	38.	H452
3.	A8312	21.	H1547	39.	H614
4.	A3526	22.	A9660/1	40.	A9626
5.	A79	23.	A4142/61	41.	A9625
6.	A9643	24.	Ag15	42.	A8868/1
7.	A9659	25.	A9628	43.	H1172
8.	A6779	26.	A69	44.	H999
9.	A6399	27.	A9427	45.	A4142/62
10.	N9/08	28.	Ag56/1	46.	H1464
11.	A8961	29.	Ag53	47.	A5502
12.	A8864	30.	Ag57	48.	A956
13.	A5503	31.	Ag71	49.	A9566
14.	Ag8	32.	A3334	50.	Ag47
15.	A9644	33.	A6893/1	51.	A2780
16.	W9/03	34.	A4244	52.	A8977
17.	A9645	35.	A2795	53.	A3943
18.	A7706	36.	Ag45	54.	A5514